GOD'S KINGDOM AND YOU!

A Child's Guide to Understanding the Bible and God's
Dream for Each Person

by Karen Price

TRILOGY

God's Kingdom and You! A Child's Guide to Understanding the Bible and God's Dream for Each Person

Trilogy Christian Publishers A Wholly Owned Subsidiary of Trinity Broadcasting Network

2442 Michelle Drive Tustin, CA 92780

Trilogy Christian Publishing/TBN and colophon are trademarks of Trinity Broadcasting Network.

Cover design by: Natalee Dunning

For information about special discounts for bulk purchases, please contact Trilogy Christian Publishing.

Trilogy Disclaimer: The views and content expressed in this book are those of the author and may not necessarily reflect the views and doctrine of Trilogy Christian Publishing or the Trinity Broadcasting Network.

Manufactured in the United States of America

10 9 8 7 6 5 4 3 2 1

Library of Congress Cataloging-in-Publication Data is available.
ISBN: 978-1-63769-556-2
E-ISBN: 978-1-63769-557-9

DEDICATION

To Timothy James, my first grandchild.

PREFACE

This book was written to help children understand the valuable place they have in God's Kingdom.

As I listened to Myles Munroe on TV and read some of his books (including *Rediscovering the Kingdom* and *The Most Important Person on Earth*), I regretted I had not learned Kingdom principles in my childhood.

I could not find any materials written for children, so I began writing my own lesson plans. I read just a few pages to them at one sitting. The next time we met, we reviewed or reread that material before progressing. I found the children quickly memorized the words (even if they could not read) and comprehended the concepts. There are no chapters or other divisions in this book—just place a bookmark where you want to pick up again.

The Scripture references are placed at the back of the book for further Bible study.

Also, thanks to Don and Micki Milam for writing the grace-filled book, *The Ancient Language of Eden*, and Don Nori of Destiny Image Publishers for inspiring me with his talk on the Miracle Channel about God's dream for each of us.

Enjoy!

GOD'S KINGDOM AND YOU!

In the beginning, God created the heavens and the earth.

> That means He made everything out of nothing.
> Everything you see and everything you cannot see,
> God created it all.

> At first, everything was dark and quiet.
> The Holy Spirit was moving above the waters.

Then God spoke.

> When God speaks, things happen!
> Life and order come.

God said, *"Light."*

> Light appeared,
> *And God saw that it was good.*
> That means He approved.

> God separated the light from darkness.
> God called the light *day,* and
> He called the darkness *night.*

> Evening passed, morning came. It was *day one.*

This was the beginning of time—on earth.
There is no time in heaven.

God said, *"Waters, separate."*

> God made the *sky* and separated the waters
> above the sky from the waters below the sky.

Evening passed, morning came. It was *day two.*

∞

God said, *"Waters below the sky, come together.*
Land, appear."

> Immediately dry ground appeared,
> and God called it *land.*

> The waters that had come together
> He called *seas.*
> *And God saw that it was good.*

> Then God said, *"Land, produce plants."*
> And it was so.

> There were plants that had seeds.
> There were trees that had fruit with
> seeds inside the fruit.
> Each seed grew its own kind of plant.
> *And God saw that it was good.*

Evening passed, morning came. It was *day three.*

∞

God said, *"Lights, come and shine!"*

God made the sun to be in charge of the day
and the moon to be in charge of the night.

Then He added all the stars.
God said these lights would be signs
to mark seasons and days and years.
And God saw that it was good.

Evening passed, morning came. It was *day four.*

⚬⚬⚬

God said, *"Waters, be filled with sea life.
Birds, fly in the air."*

So, God made the large sea animals,
such as the whales and dolphins,
and every living thing in the water.

He also made every bird that flies.
And God saw that it was good.

God *blessed* them and said,
"Have many young ones, so you will be many."
That means a whale will have baby whales,
and a sparrow will have baby sparrows.

Evening passed, morning came. It was *day five.*

⚬⚬⚬

God said, *"Earth, be filled with animals."*
So God made wild animals,
tame animals,
and animals that crawl—
reptiles, mice, and bugs—
and told them to have more young.

And God saw that it was good.

Then…

God said, *"Let Us*
[meaning the Father, Son, and Holy Spirit]
make man in Our image,
after Our likeness, and
let them have complete responsibility
—over the fish in the sea,
—the birds in the sky,
—the tame animals,
—over all the earth, and
—over all the creatures that move
along the ground."

What does this mean?

Before we answer that question,
we first need to talk about God.

Who is God?

The word *God* describes a being who needs nothing
or no one to exist. He has always lived.

That means there was no beginning to God
and there will be no end to God.
He was never born and will never die.
No one else can claim that.

God is Spirit. That means we can't see Him.
God never changes. He is already perfect.

God is All-Powerful. That is called *Omnipotent.*
God is All-Knowing. That is called *Omniscient.*
God is Everywhere. That is called *Omnipresent.*

So the God of the Bible is the Only One
who truthfully can be called God.

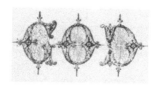

Since God has always existed,
>   we don't know when He created heaven.
>   Heaven is the world we can't see
>   —the invisible world—
>   that is somewhere above the sky.

What is heaven like?
>   Try to picture—
>   the most beautiful colors,
>   the most beautiful music,
>   the most beautiful flowers and grass—

Heaven is even more beautiful than that!

>   Everything is bright, light, happy, and relaxed.
>   There is much laughter and joy.

>   *What does God do in heaven?*

God is King!

That means He is in charge of heaven.

In heaven, God the *Father,* God the *Son,*
>   and God the *Holy Spirit* were together,
>   enjoying this wonderful place.

But there is more to heaven!

There are angels in heaven!

God created many groups of angels.
They all worship and serve God.

They never get discouraged and never give up.
They never die.
And, most importantly, they *only* listen to God.

One group delights in praising the name of the Lord.
They never get tired of worshiping God.
This group is called the *Seraphim.*
    They have six wings:
        two that cover the face,
            two that cover the feet,
                and two for flying.

There is a group that guards God's throne.
They are called the *Cherubim.*
    They are beautiful and have four wings
        and are covered with beautiful stones.

There is a group called *Ministering Angels.*
    God sends them out to help and protect.

Some angels are *Messengers.*
    They deliver special information from God.

Only three angels are called by their names in the Bible:
Michael, Gabriel, and Lucifer.

Sometimes angels appear to people.
Then they might look like a person,
but maybe bigger and stronger.

As wonderful as angels are, they always worship God.
We are never, never, never to worship angels.

~REMEMBER~

We are to worship only God!

Sadly, one group of angels decided to rebel against God.
That means they did not want to obey God.
They did not want to worship God.

The leader became proud and wanted
to take over God's position in heaven.

Why was he proud?

He was in love with his own beauty.
Since he was one of the *Cherubim,*
he was covered with beautiful stones.

His job was to guard God's throne.
But now he wanted to sit on that throne
and be worshiped—instead of God.

He said, "I will go up to heaven and put my throne
above God's stars. I will be like God."

Who was this leader?

Satan, the devil.
Yes, Satan was once the angel Lucifer in heaven.

But now he and one-third of the other angels
who joined him had to leave their Creator
and their wonderful home in heaven.

That means one group of angels went with Satan,
but two groups of angels stayed with God.

Only love and light could be in heaven.
Satan and his angels chose to let evil come inside
and cover them like a blanket of darkness.

Satan and his angels will never return to heaven.

Since Satan cannot return to heaven,
　　his plan is to deceive or trick others
　　　　so they won't get to enjoy heaven either.

　To trick people, sometimes he changes himself
　　to look like a good angel.

　Satan even uses well-meaning people to work his plans.
　That means he sometimes uses nice people to
　talk others into serving Satan instead of God.

God had to make a new eternal home
　　for Satan and his angels—it is called hell.
　　It is a place of burning fire.

　Someday Satan and his angels will be sent there,
　　and they will live there forever.

　　Just like heaven is forever,
　　　hell is also forever.
　　No one ever dies in heaven or in hell.

The Bible says, *"God is love."*
　　That means everything He does comes from love.
　　Heaven is filled with love everywhere.
　　There can't be any darkness or evil in heaven.

　　God's love was so great,
　　He wanted to share that love even more!

God decided to bring heaven's Kingdom to a new world.
He would have to create that new world.

And so He did. He created a world filled with
land and seas,
days and nights,
sun, moon, and stars,
fish, birds, and animals.

But He wasn't through yet.

His final and best creation was yet to come.

When God said, *"Let Us make man in Our image,"*
that meant God wanted to create man
to have the same loving, caring nature that He has.

It was important that man be kind and loving because
God was going to give him the big responsibility of
taking care of the earth with the same loving care
that God takes care of heaven.

God was going to be very creative!

The creation of man was very different
    from the creation of the animals and birds.

Man was going to be able to make choices.
    He would choose to love God, or
        he would choose not to love God.

God knew this was risky because all of His love
    and careful creation might be rejected by man.

In His great wisdom, God already had a plan
    just in case man would choose not to love Him.

∽∾

Now God was ready!
He took some dirt from the ground and made a body…
    a body with eyes, ears, arms, and legs just like you have.

But this body couldn't move yet—it had no life.

Then God breathed into man, and man became alive!

When God breathed into man,
that made man different from all the animals.

With that breath,
God gave man a spirit and a soul.

Man's *spirit* is the part that talks with God.
Man's *soul* is the part that thinks and makes decisions.
Man's *body* is the outside part that needs
    good food, water, and sleep to stay strong.

God named this man *Adam.*

God was very happy to have man to take care of this
 spectacular world He had created.

God began to talk with Adam using words.
 In heaven, words aren't necessary—just thoughts.

God placed Adam eastward
 in the beautiful Garden of Eden,
 a place created especially for him.

God blessed Adam and told him to
 have children to fill this wonderful world,
 take responsibility over all the earth,
 use all the resources wisely,
 be in charge of all the animals,
 and use the plants for food.

(But God never told Adam to rule over other people.)

Since Adam was now in charge of the earth,
 God brought all the birds and animals to
 him so he could give each one a name.

As Adam looked at each one, he thought of the
 perfect name for each bird and each animal.

Remember, Adam was creative in
 his choice of names because
 he was created to think like God!

In the center of this beautiful garden were two special trees:
—*The Tree of Life* and
—*The Tree of the Knowledge of Good and Evil*

God had only one rule for Adam:

*"You may eat of every tree in the Garden
except the Tree of the Knowledge of Good and Evil.
If you eat of that tree, you will die."*

Why did God make the "rule"?

Remember when God made Adam?
God created him to be able to choose.
Adam chose names for the birds and animals.
Now he has another choice to make.

Is Adam going to obey God?

Then God said, *"It is not good for Adam to be alone. I will make a helper suitable for him."*

We don't know if Adam felt lonely and wanted another person to be with him in the Garden.

But God knew.

⁓REMEMBER⁓

God always knows what is best for us!

We are about to see God's creativity again...
and the first surgery—without a hospital!
God put Adam into a deep sleep.
Then God took out part of a bone from Adam's side
and made it into a woman.

Then God brought her to Adam!
Imagine Adam's excitement at seeing this wonderful person God made—just for him! Adam said,
"This is now bone of my bone,
and flesh of my flesh.
She shall be called woman,
because she was taken out of man."

Adam called this woman Eve,
and they became the first husband and wife.

God had created the first family on earth!

Now Adam could share this spectacular home,
      the Garden of Eden, with his beautiful wife, Eve.

Imagine Eve seeing for the first time—
    gigantic palm trees,
      delicate ferns,
        tall giraffes,
          fluffy rabbits,
            comical penguins,
              majestic eagles,

feeling the soft green grass on her toes,
    splashing sparkling water on Adam,
      marveling at the starry sky at night,
        smelling the fragrance of the flowers.

Everything was perfect!

    God was so happy.

He saw everything He had made,

    and indeed it was very good!

Evening passed, morning came. It was *day six.*

By day seven, God had finished all His creating.

It was finished down to the last detail.

On the seventh day, God rested.
God blessed the seventh day.

God made the seventh day holy.
He rested from all His creating.

The seventh day was also Adam and Eve's first day.
Their first day began in the rest of God.
There was no hurry, no worry—just peace and love.

The days following were just as special
        as being in heaven.

*That's because heaven had come to earth—
        just as God had planned, just as He had dreamed.*

The big difference between heaven and earth
        was that Adam was in charge of earth,
                just as God is in charge of heaven.

∽

God also gave Adam the responsibility
        to take care of the Garden.

Adam and God had such a close friendship
        that Adam knew what needed to be done
                and how God wanted the Garden to look.

Adam and Eve didn't even have to water the plants!
God had the first automatic sprinkler system—a mist
        came out of the ground and watered everything!

There was also a river in the Garden of Eden,
        but there wasn't any rain. It wasn't needed.
Everything was perfect!

In the cool of the day, Adam and Eve
        enjoyed walking and talking with God.
Everything was perfect!

Adam and Eve were living God's dream for them!

One day, Eve was talking with a serpent, a snake. Perhaps she had talked with him before—we don't know—but she did not seem surprised to see him or to be talking with an animal.

But this wasn't an ordinary snake. Remember how Satan had lost his position in heaven? We don't know exactly when that happened. It might have been after Satan saw how wonderful the Garden of Eden was and how much God enjoyed being with Adam and Eve. We do know Satan was jealous of God and wanted to take over God's throne. Satan chose to let evil come inside him and could no longer stay in heaven. And Satan couldn't come to the Garden either because no evil was allowed there.

Now he wanted to trick Adam and Eve so they wouldn't be able to enjoy the Garden or God's presence any longer. So, Satan borrowed the body of a snake so he could sneak into the Garden and talk with Eve.

The serpent asked her, *"Did God really say you are not to eat from any tree in the Garden?"*

Eve's first mistake was answering Satan.
She should have told him to just leave her alone,
and he would have left her immediately;
in fact, he would have run away from her.

Instead, Eve answered Satan, *"We may eat fruit from the trees in the Garden, but God said we are not to eat fruit from the tree that is in the middle of the Garden and we are not to touch it, or we will die."*

Is that what God said? Let's read it again:

*"You may eat of every tree in the Garden except
the Tree of the Knowledge of Good and Evil.
If you eat of that tree, you will die."*

What did Eve add to God's "rule"?

⁓REMEMBER⁓

Never change what God has said.

God did not say, "Do not touch the fruit" —
     He said, "Do not eat it."

Then the serpent said to Eve,
     *"You won't die. God knows that when you eat the fruit,
     your eyes will be opened, and you will be like God, knowing
     good and evil."*

After hearing that, Eve chose to let doubt come in her heart.
She forgot that she was already like God.
But she did not know what evil was—God wanted to forever
protect her from that. Now she began not to trust God
and His dream for her.

Then she *looked* at the fruit and began to *want* it.
She took some and *ate* it. Nothing happened.

Then she gave some to her husband, Adam, *and he ate it.*
Then things happened.

You see, when God made Adam and breathed into him, the Holy Spirit came inside Adam to live and give Adam constant communication with God. That means any time Adam had a question, he could immediately talk to God about it.

We don't know why Adam didn't talk to God as soon as Eve ate the fruit. Adam must have told Eve about the "rule." Adam should have said, *"No, Eve, don't eat it. God said not to."* But, more importantly, Adam knew better, and *he* should not have eaten it.

If Adam had not eaten the fruit,
perhaps everything still
would be perfect.

─REMEMBER─

Always choose to do what is right,
even if others choose not to.

Adam and Eve both chose to separate themselves from God and to become independent and reject God's dream for them.

Now God couldn't trust them to take care of the Garden of Eden because they had chosen to listen to God's enemy, Satan.

God had to do something very hard and very sad.

God had to remove Adam and Eve from the Garden of Eden.

God had said that they would die.
That didn't mean their bodies would immediately die.

But it did mean that the Holy Spirit would leave.
No longer would Adam and Eve have constant
communication with God.

And now, instead of living forever, like God,
their bodies would slowly start to die.

No longer was life perfect.

No longer did they have the Holy Spirit
giving them a glory covering from the inside out.

Now they had only their five natural senses:
    sight
    hearing
    touch
    smell
    taste

They looked with their eyes—*the glory was gone*—
        and they saw their bodies uncovered.

They became afraid—something they had never felt before—
and made some clothes out of leaves from a plant.

They even tried to hide from God.

Do you think they could really hide from God?
Of course not. God knew exactly where they were.

When God asked Adam and Eve if they had disobeyed the "rule," they started playing the blame game.
Have you ever played the blame game?

Adam said, *"It's Eve's fault.*
She gave me some fruit, and I ate it."

God asked Eve, *"Is this what you have done?"*
Can you guess what Eve said?
"The serpent deceived me, and I ate."

God said to the serpent, *"Because you did this, a curse will be put on you. I will make you and the woman enemies to each other. Your descendants and her descendants will be enemies. One of her descendants will crush your head, and you will bite His heel."*

This meant that one day a Person would come who would break the power of Satan and take back the authority that Adam once held, and the Kingdom would be restored back to man!

Then God told Adam and Eve that now life would be hard. They would have to sweat and work hard to get food, and there would be pain in giving birth to children. God said the ground was cursed, and there would be weeds and thorns.

But GOD never cursed Adam and Eve.
He still loved them very much.

It was almost time for Adam and Eve to leave their wonderful home. But first, God did something very special for them. He made them clothes out of skins. Where did God get the skins? *An innocent animal had to die because of Adam and Eve's sin.*

Then God made them leave the Garden. Because God loved them so much, He had to make sure they never got back in.

If they ever ate of the Tree of Life, they would live forever in their sin...like Satan. Remember, Adam and Eve lost their place in God's Kingdom on earth—they did *not* lose their place in heaven after they died on earth.

Then God placed *cherubim* (the angels that guard) with a flaming sword to guard the border and the way to the Tree of Life.

∽

Adam and Eve walked away, feeling very alone and afraid.
The Holy Spirit was no longer inside them—
He returned to heaven because He could only live
inside people who chose to obey God.

Satan had introduced Adam and Eve to fear and death.

Now they had to work hard just to survive.
Now they no longer loved God's Kingdom the most.
Now they thought about their own kingdom
and began to dream their own dreams.

God felt sad like a parent does when a child dies.
His beloved children were gone.

God was sad, but was He surprised?

Do you remember what we read on page 12?
> *God made man to be able to make choices.*
> *In His great wisdom, God had a plan*
> *in case man would choose not to love Him.*

Also, God had given Adam responsibility over the earth—
God did not go back on His Word.

God still owned the earth, but He let Adam and all future people continue to be in charge of the earth, except for the Garden of Eden. But now, God would only help *if* the people asked Him to help.

God already told Satan what would happen in the future. Since Satan once was one of God's angels, he understood very well. Satan knew that someday someone would be born who would bring back the Holy Spirit to earth again.

But Satan didn't know who it would be or when.
> So he did his best to make the world very wicked.
> He tricked the people to get them to do wrong things.
> He tried to kill the people who loved God.

Now Satan was in charge of the earth—
> because Adam and Eve had listened to him.

∼∽∾∽

But God had a plan!

God's plan was to make a way for the Holy Spirit to come back and live inside people who would love Him and serve Him willingly.

It would end up taking 4,000 years for this to happen.

The Old Testament tells about those 4,000 years.

It started with *Adam and Eve*. They must have taught their children about loving God because one son, *Abel*, brought a gift to God that pleased God. His brother, *Cain*, brought an offering that God did not accept. Cain became jealous of Abel and killed him. This was the first murder on earth.

Later the world became so wicked that God had *Noah*, who loved and served God, build a big boat so he and his family and a pair of every animal could be saved while God destroyed the rest of the people on the earth in a flood.

> *Then God put a beautiful rainbow in the sky*
> *as His promise to never again destroy*
> *the whole world in a flood.*

But after a while, the people again became so proud; they decided to build a tall tower that would reach far into the sky. Since they all spoke the same language, it was easy for them to work together and make it happen.

God saw that they would be able to do anything they wanted because they spoke the same language.

God decided to confuse them so they couldn't understand each other. Soon they had to give up their project. God caused them to scatter all around the world.

Later on, God used *Abraham, Isaac, and Jacob* to keep His plan, His dream, moving forward.

Beginning with *Abraham*, God again gave a *blessing* to the nations through Abraham. It was similar to the blessing God had given Adam many years earlier. God taught Abraham about giving offerings that included killing *innocent animals* when asking God to forgive their sins.

Remember, God is love, and He had a plan to bring His Kingdom to earth again.

Abraham had a son promised by God named *Isaac*. Then Isaac had two sons, *Jacob* and *Esau*. God chose *Jacob* to continue the line for the Messiah, the One who would restore God's Kingdom to earth. God changed Jacob's name to *Israel*, which means *"prince with God."* Jacob had twelve sons who became known as the twelve tribes of Israel.

Now, God's plan continued onward for many years through this one family line. These people were called the *Hebrews* or *Israelites*. Today we know them as the *Jewish* or *Israeli* people.

Each of the Israelite children and grandchildren was reminded that the Messiah would come, and through Him, all nations would be blessed. However, the Israelites began to think they were the only ones God wanted to save and bless, and they forgot that God wanted to save and bless all people.

Even so, God used people such as *Moses, David, Isaiah, and Daniel* to tell the people about the Messiah, the King, who was coming.

As people turned to God, the Holy Spirit would come *upon* individuals for a time, but the Holy Spirit was not yet *in* people as He had been *in* Adam and Eve.

And every time people called out to God, He was there to help them, heal them, and keep them safe from evil. *But He couldn't help them unless they asked.* And after a while, they would forget about God and serve Satan again. Over and over again, the Israelites went back and forth, first serving God, then serving Satan.

It wasn't time yet.

Then the Israelites wanted to be like other nations and have a king over them. God was sad that they no longer wanted *Him* to be their unseen King.

But God let them have their wishes and had the prophet *Samuel* anoint *Saul* to be their first earthly king. Sadly, Saul disobeyed God to the point God had to remove him. Then God chose *David* to be king. David was a good king and a mighty warrior who loved God. He was also a poet and worshiper and wrote most of the *Psalms* (which means "Songs")—the longest book in the Bible. God also told him that his kingdom would never end.

What could that mean?

Other kings followed. Some loved God; most did not. Finally, the Israelite tribes were taken captive by other nations and removed from their homes.

But God did not leave His people without hope.

God gave His people a peek into the future through His prophet, *Isaiah*, who wrote:

> For unto us a Child is born, Unto us a Son is given, And the government will be upon His shoulders. And He will be called Wonderful, Counselor, Mighty God, Everlasting Father, Prince of Peace. Of the increase of His government and peace there will be no end.
>
> Isaiah 9:6-7 (NKJV)

Another prophet, *Micah*, recorded:

> But you, Bethlehem Ephrathah, [ef'-ra-tha] though you are too small to be among the army groups from Judah, from you will come One who will rule Israel for Me. He comes from very old times, from days long ago.
>
> Micah 5:2 (NCV)

Isaiah also told the people that a messenger would come first to announce this special arrival:

> This is the voice of one who calls out: prepare in the desert the way for the Lord. Make a straight road in the dry lands for our God.
>
> Isaiah 40:3 (NCV)

Do you know who this messenger is?

We'll find out soon!

There were many other interesting prophecies that hinted towards the future:

—a King entering Jerusalem on a colt
—a close friend betraying Him
—His hands and feet pierced
—wounded and whipped by His enemies
—sold for thirty pieces of silver
—spit on and beaten
—silent before His accusers, crucified with thieves

Do you know who this person is? We'll find out soon!

Later it seemed God had forgotten His people as 400 years went by with no one hearing any word from Him.

Do you think God had forgotten?

No, of course not!

God had a plan!

God still had a dream!

We don't know everything that God was waiting for, but finally, a government was in control that was formed somewhat like God's government when He created the world.

It was called the *Roman Empire.*

When Rome invaded and conquered (that means it took over) a country, it let the people stay in that country. Before that time, all the other nations took the people away from their own homes to live in another country.

Instead, Rome sent a leader, called a *governor,* to that country to be in charge over the people and teach them to speak the language of the Romans, dress like the Romans, and pay taxes to the Roman government.

The Roman Empire became so large it controlled most of the known world. Part of the reason it was so successful was that it let the people remain in their own countries.

So everywhere you went, you found Romans.
The Roman Empire was ruled by a *king.*
There were coins stamped with the king's image.

Now, it was time!

One day while a priest named *Zechariah* was worshiping God in the temple, an angel appeared to him. Zechariah was afraid when he saw the angel.

The angel said:

> Zechariah, don't be afraid. God has heard your prayer. Your wife, Elizabeth, will give birth to a son, and you will name him John. He will bring you joy and gladness, and many people will be happy because of his birth. John will be a great man for the Lord. He will never drink wine or beer, and even from birth, he will be filled with the Holy Spirit. He will help many people of Israel return to the Lord their God. He will go before the Lord in the spirit and power like Elijah. He will make peace between parents and their children and will bring those who are not obeying God back to the right way of thinking, to make a people ready for the coming of the Lord.

Luke 1:13-17 (NCV)

That sounds like what Isaiah said about the messenger. Could John be that messenger?

Zechariah and Elizabeth were old and had no children, so it seemed impossible that they would now have a child.

Zechariah asked, *"How can I know that what you say is true?"*

The angel answered,

> I am Gabriel. I stand before God, who sent me to talk to you and to tell you this good news. Now, listen! You will not be able to speak until the day these things happen because you did not believe what I told you. But they will really happen.

Luke 1:18-20 (NCV)

Wow! After 400 years of silence, God had spoken through His angel, Gabriel. But Zechariah couldn't tell anyone about his incredible experience—he couldn't speak. So he made signs to let them know what had happened.

Why do you think God didn't want Zechariah to speak? Could it be so he wouldn't say the wrong thing?

~REMEMBER~

What we speak is very important—
we must speak words that are in
agreement with God's Word.

This was no time for Zechariah to let doubt come into his heart and out through his mouth!

God had just shared with Zechariah
His dream for Zechariah and Elizabeth
and His dream for their son, John.

Did you know God has a dream for you, too?

The Bible says God had your whole life planned and written in His Book before you were even born! He has dreamed a dream for every baby. And as long as that person is alive, God has a dream for him or her (even if they are as old as Zechariah and Elizabeth!).

After you were born, God placed His dream into your heart. Maybe you already have a desire to do something. Start talking to God about it. And then get quiet and listen as He talks to you. Be ready to accept His dream for you. His dream will make you very happy and excited.

~REMEMBER~
*Obedience is doing
what God dreamed for you.*

Do you think John will do what God dreamed for him?

This was such an exciting time. Finally—after so many years—Elizabeth was going to have a baby! Zechariah somehow must have let Elizabeth know about Gabriel's visit and God's dream for them and their baby John. Maybe he wrote it down for her.

It takes about nine months for a human baby to develop inside the mother before it is time to be born. That's a long time for Zechariah to have to remain quiet!

John was in his sixth month of development when something exciting happened.

Gabriel was sent on another mission!

This time *Gabriel* went to Nazareth to see *Mary*, a young woman who was engaged to be married to a man named *Joseph*.

> Greetings! The Lord has blessed you and is with you. (Mary was startled to see an angel and hear this unusual greeting.) Don't be afraid, Mary; God has shown you His grace. Listen! You will become pregnant and give birth to a Son, and you will name Him Jesus. He will be great and will be called the Son of the Most High. The Lord God will give Him the throne of King David, His ancestor. He will rule over the people of Jacob forever, and His kingdom will never end.
>
> Luke 1:28-33 (NCV)

Gabriel went on to explain how this would happen since Mary and Joseph weren't married yet:

> The Holy Spirit will come upon you, and the power of the Most High will cover you. For this reason the baby will be holy and will be called the Son of God. Now Elizabeth, your relative, is also pregnant with a son though she is very old. Everyone thought she could not have a baby, but she has been pregnant for six months. God can do anything!
>
> Luke 1:35-37 (NCV)

Listen carefully to Mary's response:
"I am the servant of the Lord.
Let this happen to me as you say!"

How is Mary's response different from Zechariah's?

Mary's words agreed with God's words
as spoken by His angel Gabriel.

God was pleased that Mary would accept His dream for her. In fact, Mary was so excited she went quickly to see Elizabeth. As she greeted Elizabeth, baby John inside Elizabeth jumped for joy, and *Elizabeth was filled with the Holy Spirit.*

How could this be? Remember the Holy Spirit went back to heaven after Adam and Eve sinned?

The baby inside Mary was brought to her
by the Holy Spirit from God the Father in heaven.

God had sent His Son to be born as a baby and live as a man —just like Adam had lived—only without any sin.
The Holy Spirit is back on earth again!

Now life is getting very exciting!

Why do you think baby John jumped when Mary came? An unborn baby hears what is going on and can respond. John heard the Holy Spirit in Mary, and somehow he knew something special had happened. Perhaps that was the moment he was filled with the Holy Spirit. He was excited!

As soon as Elizabeth saw Mary and she felt John jump for joy, the Holy Spirit told Elizabeth that Mary was going to have the Christ Child that had been promised long ago when Satan tricked Adam and Eve in the Garden of Eden.

Elizabeth blessed Mary for believing God and not doubting His Word to her.

Then Mary praised God with her voice,
thanking Him for what He had done.

∽

Three months passed, and Elizabeth gave birth to her long-awaited son. Even though Elizabeth said his name would be John, their relatives thought he should be named after his father, Zechariah.

Finally, Zechariah wrote on paper, *"His name is John."* When he wrote that, he *immediately* could talk. Perhaps writing John's name showed he finally agreed with God's dream and Gabriel's announcement.

Now Zechariah began to praise God. The neighbors became very respectful of God and wondered what John would be when he grew up because they could tell he was special.

Zechariah was also filled with the Holy Spirit and began to tell what John's future would be like. He said,

> Now you, child, will be called a prophet of the Most High God. You will go before the Lord to prepare his way. You will make His people know that they will be saved by having their sins forgiven. With the loving mercy of our God, a new day from heaven will dawn upon us.

Luke 1:76-78 (NCV)

John was indeed chosen by God to be the messenger that Isaiah had told about many years earlier. God's dream for John was that he would prepare the way for the Son of God. Will John accept God's dream for him? And how will he prepare the way?

Zechariah and Elizabeth took care of baby John and raised him according to the instruction of the angel Gabriel.

∞

In the meantime, what was happening with Mary and Baby Jesus? Joseph didn't understand what was taking place, so one night, an angel came to him in a dream:

> Joseph, descendant of David, don't be afraid to take Mary as your wife, because the baby in her is from the Holy Spirit. She will give birth to a Son, and you will name Him Jesus, because He will save His people from their sins.
>
> Matthew 1:20-21 (NCV)

When Joseph woke up, he knew it was right to take Mary as his wife and to love and raise *Jesus* as the promised Savior of the world.

Notice, the angel reminded Joseph that he was a descendant of David. The angel Gabriel had also told Mary that God would give Jesus the throne of David and there will be no end to His Kingdom. Do you remember we read on page 28 that many years earlier, God had told King David there would be no end to his kingdom? Now we know this meant Jesus would come! No doubt Joseph grew up knowing about God's promise to his ancestor David. Now Joseph realized God had dreamed a dream for him, too—to be the step-father of the Son of God!

When six months had passed, it was almost time for Jesus to be born. But first, Joseph and Mary had to travel to Bethlehem to be counted as citizens.

Remember, the Roman government let them live in their own country, but they still had to be counted and pay taxes to Rome.

While they were there, it was definitely time for Jesus to be born—soon! In fact, that night! Since so many people were in Bethlehem, there wasn't any place to spend the night.

So, Jesus was born in a barn. It was probably not very pretty or sweet-smelling. But it was filled with love. Mary wrapped her baby in *swaddling cloths*—those were strips of cloth she had in her traveling bag. *(Swaddling cloths were used to wrap the arms and legs of a baby to keep them growing straight. These cloths were also used to wrap a person who had died.)*

That very night shepherds were outside watching over their sheep. An angel of the Lord stood before them. The glory of God was shining around them, and they were afraid.

But the angel said:

> Do not be afraid, I am bringing you good news that will be a great joy to all the people. Today your Savior was born in the town of David. He is Christ the Lord. This is how you will know Him: You will find a Baby wrapped in pieces of cloth and lying in a feeding box.

Luke 2:10-12 (NCV)

Then a very large group of angels from heaven joined the first angel, praising God and saying:

"Give glory to God in heaven, and on earth let there be peace among the people who please God."

After the angels left them and went back to heaven, the shepherds said to each other,

"Let's see this thing that has happened, which the Lord has told us about."

⁓

How do you think you would have felt if an angel had given you this message?
Would you have believed it?
Would you have hurried to Bethlehem?
Would you have known where to look for the baby?
Would you have told others?

⁓

These shepherds hurried, found Baby Jesus, and told Mary and Joseph about their visit by the angels. Mary listened carefully and often thought about what they said. She probably reminded herself again about her own visit from Gabriel. And Joseph likely thought about his special visit with an angel in a dream.

The shepherds went back to their sheep, praising God for what had happened—exactly as the angel had said.

Life is very exciting right now!

Do you remember that the prophet Micah had said One would come from Bethlehem? Even though it was hard for Mary and Joseph to have to travel to Bethlehem and stay in a stable, God used this hard time to bring about His perfect will.

~REMEMBER~

God will work every detail
into something good
if we love Him and obey Him.

Because Jesus was their first son, Mary and Joseph took Him to Jerusalem to the temple (that's like a church) to offer Him to the Lord, along with an offering of a pair of doves or pigeons. Wealthy people offered a lamb plus a dove or pigeon.

In the temple court was an elderly man, *Simeon*, who loved and served God. He knew he would not die until he had seen *Christ*. The Holy Spirit led him to the temple court the very day Mary and Joseph came with Jesus—and Simeon took Jesus in his arms and praised God for he knew he had now seen Christ.

In the temple was an elderly woman, *Anna*, and she also came up to them and gave thanks to God for this child.

There was no doubt Jesus was the Messiah!

Something else happened about this time. Some wise men from the East came to Jerusalem asking where the newborn king of the Jews was. They explained they had observed a star in the eastern sky that signaled His birth, and they had come to worship Him.

You can imagine that Herod, King of Judea, did *not* like hearing that! He quickly asked his own advisors if this could be true. They knew what the prophet Micah had written and said, *"Yes, in Bethlehem."*

King Herod asked the wise men when they had first seen the star and then told them to go to Bethlehem:

"Look carefully for the child. When you find Him, come tell me so I can worship Him, too."

Do you think King Herod really wanted to worship Jesus?
What idea do you think Satan put in his heart?

Remember, Satan knew that someday One would be born who would restore the Holy Spirit to earth. He just didn't know Who or when it would be.

The wise men didn't have to search for Jesus—the star appeared again and traveled in the sky above them. Then it stopped right where Jesus was now living with his parents!

When the men saw Jesus, they bowed, actually fell to the ground, and worshiped Him. And they gave Him special gifts—gifts given to kings.

Gold—nuggets from the ground.

Frankincense—white resin from a tree. When burned, it gives off a sweet smell.

Myrrh—also a resin cut from a tree. It was used as a perfume, especially for the dead.

What had King Herod told the wise men to do after they found the child? But the wise men did not go back and tell King Herod *because they were warned by God in a dream.* So they returned to their home another way.

After the wise men had gone, an angel appeared to Joseph in a dream and said,

"Get up! Take the child and His mother and escape to Egypt because Herod is starting to look for the child so he can kill Him. Stay in Egypt until I tell you to return."

So that very night, Joseph left quickly and quietly with Mary and Jesus and went to Egypt. They stayed in Egypt until Herod died.

Do you think God had the wise men give Jesus gold so it could be used for money while they stayed in Egypt?

It didn't take long for King Herod to get suspicious when the wise men didn't return to Jerusalem. He had already killed some of his own sons because he was afraid they wanted to take over his kingdom, so now he decided to kill all boys ages two and younger. It was a sad day for many mothers. But Jesus was safe. *Satan lost again.*

Then Joseph had another dream, and this time the angel told him to return to Israel to live because Herod was now dead. When they arrived in Israel, Joseph was afraid of the new king (Herod's son). Joseph was warned in yet another dream and traveled north to Galilee, where they settled in Nazareth.

Jesus became known as Jesus of Nazareth, the son of *Joseph* (who was his earthly step-father). Joseph was a carpenter, and we can be certain that Jesus grew up learning how to work with tools and make things because later He became known as a carpenter also. His parents had four other sons and some daughters. It must have been a happy family with at least seven children.

Jesus grew strong in body and wise in spirit, and the grace of God was on Him. Mary and Joseph took very good care of Jesus and taught Him well. In fact, once, when He was twelve years old, He amazed the teachers in the temple with His great understanding.

Not far away, Elizabeth and Zechariah were also taking good care of their son, John, and teaching him well.

Life for Jesus and John must have been a happy, fun childhood with much learning, growing, and obeying their parents.

∽

Now it was time for *John* to fulfill God's dream for him. Do you remember what it was? (Look back at page 32.)

When John became an adult, he began to tell the people:

> There is One coming who is greater than I. I am not good enough even to kneel down and untie His sandals. I baptize you with water, but He will baptize you with the Holy Spirit.
>
> Mark 1:7-8 (NCV)

People came and listened to John. They confessed their sins and were baptized by John in the Jordan River. John knew he was fulfilling God's dream *by preparing the way for Jesus.* He was getting the people ready. He was the *announcer,* one who says, "May I now introduce to you my good friend." Only John said it this way,

> Look, the Lamb of God, who takes away the sin of the world! This is the One I was talking about when I said, A man will come after me, but He is greater than I am, because He was living before me...I tell you the truth: This man is the Son of God.
>
> John 1:29-30, 34 (NCV)

He started telling people, *"Change your life. God's Kingdom is here."*

People came from far and near to hear him and to see him. Perhaps they wanted to see his unusual clothing made out of camel's hair or the unusual food he ate—locusts and honey!

God's dream for John was that he would prepare the people to be ready to hear Jesus. John would seem somewhat like the prophet Elijah—that's probably why he dressed like Elijah and ate unusual foods. John was to bring the people back to the right way of thinking.

So when John said, *"Change your life. God's Kingdom is here,"* the people confessed their sins and were baptized in water.

That means the people changed their way of doing things and decided to follow John's way. Then their baptism in water let everyone know they had committed themselves to follow John's teachings.

Getting baptized in water feels like it does when you hold your breath and dunk your head under water; when you come up out of the water, you feel light, happy, and clean.

So many people were baptized by John that he became known as *John the Baptist.*

~

John knew and accepted God's dream for him—
to prepare people for the coming of Jesus.

~

Even though it would have been easy for John to want to draw people to himself so he would feel important, he *always* remembered to make sure the people knew Jesus was the most important One.

One day, Jesus came to John the Baptist and asked John to baptize Him in water. John replied, *"I'm the one who needs to be baptized by You!"*

John knew the importance of baptism—it meant people had decided to follow his teachings. So John knew *he* should be baptized by Jesus—showing others that *he* was going to follow Jesus.

But Jesus assured John it needs to be done this way. So John obeyed Jesus and baptized Him in water. Jesus was showing the people that He was joining God's Kingdom, the one that John was telling everyone about.

Something special was about to happen!

As Jesus came up out of the water, the heavens opened, and the Holy Spirit came upon Jesus like a dove. Suddenly a voice came from heaven: "This is My Son, whom I love, and I am very pleased with Him" (Matthew 3:17, NCV).

Father God was letting everyone know that Jesus was on earth to bring the Holy Spirit back to earth again—the first time since Adam and Eve had sinned in the Garden.

Then the Holy Spirit did something that may seem strange. He led Jesus to go into the wilderness where Jesus fasted (that means he went without food and drank only water) for forty days and nights. He wanted to be quiet and listen closely so He would obey Father God and not think about eating. Remember, even though Jesus was God, He did everything on earth as a human—like you or me! So, you can imagine how hungry Jesus was after forty days of not eating anything.

Then Satan came to Jesus and challenged Him with food. First, it was to turn the stones into bread *if* He was the Son of God. Even though Jesus was hungry, He told Satan that man doesn't live only on bread but on every word of God.

But Satan wasn't going to give up easily. He took Jesus to the highest point of the temple. Again, he challenged Jesus to throw Himself over the edge because His angels would catch Him in their hands.

Did you notice that this time Satan quoted the Bible? He thought he was getting tricky—just like he did with Eve.

But Jesus knew what Satan was up to. Jesus quoted another verse that said not to tempt the Lord your God.

Once more, Satan led Jesus to a very high mountain and told Jesus all the kingdoms of the world could belong to Jesus if Jesus would only bow down and worship Satan.

Satan's desires had not changed—long ago, when he was still an angel in heaven, he wanted to be worshiped.

What would have happened if Jesus had bowed down and worshiped Satan? Everything would have changed because Jesus would have turned the world over to Satan forever.

But Jesus told Satan to get away because the Bible says to worship the Lord your God and serve Him only. And Satan had to leave!

~REMEMBER~

*You are to worship the Lord God and
serve Him only. Tell Satan to get away.*

Then the angels came and ministered to Jesus. Can you imagine how happy they were that Jesus had not listened to Satan! (Otherwise, they would have had to leave, too!)

Now it was time for Jesus to begin His ministry. He was thirty years old, the age for a man to become a master teacher and have his own "school."

John had said that Jesus must become greater and that he must become less. So John knew it was time for Jesus to be in charge of all the people that John had baptized in water. That's like your school teacher letting a new teacher come in and begin teaching the students.

John had fulfilled God's dream for him. Just as we read the angel Gabriel's message about John on page 32, John had been faithful to bring the people back to the right way of thinking and to prepare them for the coming of Jesus.

∽∞∽

Will you fulfill God's dream for your life?
Take a moment and tell God that you will.

And if you don't know what His dream is,
ask Him and listen for His answer.
He wants to tell you!

∽∞∽

Now Jesus had many disciples, who were like students coming to learn about God's Kingdom. Jesus selected twelve to be full time with Him and learn about this wonderful Kingdom.

The names of the twelve disciples were:

Simon Peter, Andrew, James, John, Philip, Thomas, Matthew, James, Thaddeus, Simon, Judas, and Bartholomew.

Out of those twelve, there were three who became special friends: Peter, James, and John.

Jesus asked each of the twelve disciples to become part of His "School"—His Kingdom.

He said, "Follow Me." And they did.

⌒∞⌒

For the next three years, Jesus talked about God's Kingdom. Jesus talked to Father God to know exactly what He was to do on earth, and then He obeyed His Father exactly.

Some days Jesus taught many people.
　Some days Jesus spent time with just His disciples.
　　Some days Jesus loved and held the children.
　　Some days Jesus fed the hungry.
　　　Some days Jesus healed the sick.
　　　　Some days Jesus was very busy.
　　　　　Some days Jesus was quiet and alone.

Every day Jesus did exactly
what His Father told Him to do.

Jesus spent over three years with His students, the disciples, showing them how to live as Adam and Eve had lived in the Garden of Eden.

He showed them how to have control, or dominion, over things (not people) on the earth.

Once when there was a storm on the lake, Jesus simply said, "peace," and the wind stopped.

Another time an evil spirit had entered a boy and made him sick. Jesus calmly told the evil spirit to leave the boy and never come back. The evil spirit obeyed Jesus, and the boy was well and happy again.

Jesus taught His disciples to love and accept people, rich or poor; it didn't matter to Jesus.

Jesus also told them to love each other and not fight. He said then others would know they were part of God's Kingdom—if they were kind to each other. In fact, Jesus said the two most important "rules" are:

(1) Love God with all your heart, and
(2) Love others the way you love yourselves.

Jesus also explained many things using stories, so the disciples would remember them better.

One day the disciples asked Jesus how they should pray. He answered them with what we now call—

The Lord's Prayer

Our Father, who art in heaven,
Hallowed be Thy Name.
Thy Kingdom come.
Thy will be done in earth, as it is in heaven.
Give us this day our daily bread.
And forgive us our debts,
as we forgive our debtors.
And lead us not into temptation,
but deliver us from evil:
For Thine is the Kingdom,
and the power,
and the glory,
forever.
Amen.

Did you notice that Jesus prayed that His Father's will be done once again on earth as it is in heaven?

❦

The three years went by quickly.

Now it was almost time for Jesus to have a special talk with His disciples.

Do you know what this talk is going to be about?

Before we answer that, do you remember *why* Jesus left heaven and came to earth as a baby?

Turn back to page 23.

God told Satan that one day someone would come who would take back Satan's authority and give that authority back to the people who had the Holy Spirit inside them so they could enjoy life as Adam and Eve had enjoyed the Garden of Eden. How was this going to be?

Yes, Jesus was born as a baby and was living on earth.

But that wasn't enough.

When God had an innocent animal killed to provide clothes for Adam and Eve after they had sinned, they understood the importance of what God had done.

Adam and Eve knew that someday an innocent person would die for the sins of all the people of the world.

For 4,000 years, God's people read about someone who would die for them (see page 30).

❧

But would it have to be Jesus, the friend of the disciples? They had been together for three years—
the disciples couldn't bear the thought of seeing their friend die.

This was going to be a very difficult talk.

In those days in Israel, people wore sandals. They walked a lot on the hot, dusty sand. So when they came into a house, there was a bowl of water for them to wash the sand off their feet.

Just before the talk, Jesus washed His disciples' feet and dried them with a towel to show them how much He loved them and the kind of love they were to have for each other.

Earlier, a woman had poured expensive perfume on Jesus' feet to show Him how much she loved Him. The disciples were upset that she wasted the perfume. But Jesus said she had used the perfume for His burial.

What did that mean?

☙❧

Then came the Day of the Passover. This was the time when a special lamb was selected to be killed for all the sins of the people that year.

For 4,000 years, the people had done this once a year. It had to be a perfect lamb, not sick or weak.

After the priest had selected the perfect lamb, he brought the lamb back into Jerusalem on his shoulders so the lamb wouldn't get hurt by walking.

It was like a parade, with the people waiting along the road to see the perfect lamb that had been selected.

About this time, Jesus asked two of His disciples to go into a village and borrow a young donkey that had never been ridden. And He got on it and started to ride. Remember, He had authority over animals—so the donkey was obedient.

Do you think this is how a king would ride into town? No, but Jesus wasn't an ordinary king! He didn't have to brag by coming in a fancy chariot.

When the people heard that Jesus was coming into Jerusalem on a donkey, they took palm branches and put clothes on the ground as a carpet.

As Jesus rode by, the excited people shouted, *"Hosanna, blessed is He Who comes in the name of the Lord! Blessed is the King of Israel!"*

Wow! Do you remember on page 30? There was a hint that a King would ride into Jerusalem on a colt (donkey). Take a moment and read the rest of the prophecies on page 30.

God does everything in exactly the right time!
Jesus was the Perfect Lamb!

∽⊗∾

Now it was time for Jesus and His disciples to share their last meal together. It was called the Last Supper.

Then Jesus took a loaf of bread, prayed a prayer of thanksgiving to Father God, and gave each one a piece. *"This loaf is My body, which is now being offered to you. Always eat it to remember Me."* Then He lifted up the cup, saying, *"This cup is My blood of the new covenant I make with you, and it will be poured out soon for all of you."*

Jesus told His twelve disciples that one of them would betray Him. That means one disciple would decide no longer to be part of His Kingdom. (Do you remember Adam and Eve decided to betray God?)

Do you think the disciples looked at each other, wondering who had decided not to be Jesus' friend any longer?

Jesus also told them He would be going away. His disciples wanted to go with Him, but Jesus said they could not go with Him this time.

Jesus told them not to be sad because He was getting a place ready for them in His Father's House. Then Jesus said He would come back and take them to be with Him.

Jesus wanted the disciples to know that because they had chosen to be part of God's Kingdom, they would enjoy God's Kingdom on earth now, and when they died, they again would be with Jesus in heaven.

Then Jesus said something very important to remember:

> *"I am the Way and the Truth and the Life.*
> *No one comes to the Father except through Me."*

No doubt, the disciples were feeling confused and sad. They didn't want Jesus to leave them all alone. They didn't understand what Jesus was saying.

Then Jesus told them that Father God would send the Holy Spirit to help them. Jesus said they would be sad for a while, but later they would be happy again.

Right then, the disciples didn't feel they would ever be happy again without their friend with them.

Jesus knew it was time for Him to give up His life. He talked with His Father and said, *"Not My will but Yours be done."*

Jesus knew He had come into this world to take it from Satan, and it was now time. He chose to die.

Judas, one of the twelve disciples who traveled with Jesus full time for three years, chose to turn against Jesus. He chose not to follow the dream God had for him. And for thirty pieces of silver, Judas betrayed Jesus.

Then Jesus was arrested,
He was beaten until His body was bleeding,
and then Jesus was put on a cross
with nails in His wrists and feet.

There Jesus died—for you and me.

Jesus came to earth for this purpose. He had never done anything wrong, so He was the only person who could take all the sins—the rebellion and independence—of the people from Adam and Eve all the way forward to every baby yet to be born and *once and for all* pay the price for everybody's sins.

That means never again will a lamb have to die for the sins of the people. And that means never again will someone have to go through what Jesus did for us.

Just before Jesus died, He said, *"It is finished."*

Just like John the Baptist, Jesus had fulfilled the dream His Father God had for Him—exactly as God had told Satan in the Garden of Eden.

But do you really expect this will be the last we will hear about Jesus? No, there's much more!

After Jesus died on the cross, He was buried in a new tomb. It was a cave with a big rock that closed off the opening. (Now we understand why Jesus said the expensive perfume was for His burial.)

Suddenly after three days and three nights,
there was a big earthquake and an angel of the Lord
came and moved the large rock away.

And the tomb was empty inside!

Jesus had risen from the dead!

But where did He go?

He surprised His disciples and other friends by appearing to them. He showed them the holes in His wrists and feet so they would know He was really Jesus. They were so excited to have Jesus back with them!

Never again would Jesus have to face death!

Then Jesus breathed on His disciples and said, *"Receive the Holy Spirit."*

At last, the Holy Spirit was now inside the disciples just as He had been inside Adam and Eve when God breathed on them in the Garden of Eden. After 4,000 years, the Holy Spirit was back on earth living *inside* people! And that meant that now people would be able to talk with Father God all the time.

That's what Jesus meant when He said He would leave, but the Holy Spirit would come to help them.

But Jesus was back, too! Not for long, though.

For forty days, Jesus appeared in different places and talked with His friends, ate with them, helped them catch many fish, and told them more about the Kingdom of God.

Then one day, Jesus told His friends,

"Do not leave Jerusalem, but wait for the gift My Father promised, which you have heard Me speak about. For John baptized with water, but in a few days you will be baptized with the Holy Spirit."

Then, something amazing happened. As they watched, Jesus suddenly went up, up, up in the sky, and then a cloud hid Him from their view.

As they looked up in the sky, two men in white stood beside them and asked, *"Men of Galilee, why do you stand here looking into the sky? This same Jesus, who has been taken from you into heaven, will come back in the same way you have seen Him go into heaven."*

Jesus was gone.

But this time, the disciples were not so sad as they had been when Jesus died. Now they knew everything Jesus had told them was true.

Jesus was truly the Son of God!

And better days were ahead because Jesus told them they would soon experience the *baptism* with the Holy Spirit.

What is about to happen?

The disciples had already *received* the Holy Spirit when Jesus breathed on them.

Already the Holy Spirit was helping them feel connected
    to the Heavenly Kingdom.
Already the Holy Spirit was helping them remember the
    things Jesus had taught them.
Already the Holy Spirit was helping them not to feel sad,
    even though Jesus was gone.
Already the Holy Spirit was helping them to think and to
    talk the way Jesus wanted them to.

Can it get better than that?

Do you remember when a Roman king sent a governor to live in a country that had been conquered? The governor knew exactly what the king wanted, and he taught the people the ways of the Roman government—to dress like Romans, to act like Romans, and to learn the language of the Romans.

When the Holy Spirit came back to earth, He came as a Governor— to teach us the ways of God's Kingdom.

The Holy Spirit showed the disciples the good things they needed to have in their lives. We call these qualities *"The Fruit of the Spirit."* They are:

Love
Joy
Peace
Patience
Kindness
Goodness
Faithfulness
Gentleness
Self-control

As the disciples learned to listen to the Holy Spirit and obey His instructions, it became easier to be loving, happy, and kind to others. They began to control their tempers and were gentle with others. Just as it takes time for fruit to form on a tree, it took time for these qualities to develop in their lives.

Each disciple was now beginning to fulfill God's dream for his life!

The disciples were beginning to walk and talk and think like followers of God's Kingdom—because the Holy Spirit was *inside* them. But there was still more that the Holy Spirit was going to do in their lives!

Before *Jesus* went back to heaven to be with *God the Father*, He told His disciples they would receive *power* when the *Holy Spirit* came on them, and they would be witnesses in Jerusalem and throughout the world.

The disciples remembered John the Baptist had said Jesus would *baptize* them with the Holy Spirit (see page 44), and they also remembered the Holy Spirit had come on Jesus like a dove.

∽

What is the difference between God the Father, God the Son, and God the Holy Spirit?

You see, there are three parts of God—the Father, the Son, and the Holy Spirit. We use the word *Trinity* (that means three) or *Triune God*. It is difficult to understand, but it might help to think of water. Think of God the Father as water flowing in a beautiful river. Think of Jesus the Son as ice, which is frozen water. Think of the Holy Spirit as the steam that comes when water is boiled. Three different forms but still water.

Steam provides power to move boats or provide heat. The Holy Spirit also provides power to help the people who choose to follow God's Kingdom and already have the Holy Spirit inside them.

After Jesus had gone back to heaven, His disciples went to a big room in Jerusalem where about 120 people were praying and waiting for the Holy Spirit.

Many others had come to Jerusalem to celebrate a special feast called *Pentecost*. That word means "fifty"—and it took place exactly fifty days after a feast called *Passover* (when the priest killed a perfect lamb for the people's sins).

On the morning of Pentecost, the 120 people in that big room heard a sound. It sounded like a strong wind. They saw something like fire on the heads of the people in the room. Everyone was *baptized* with the Holy Spirit and began to speak in other languages!

There were many people from far and near in Jerusalem for the feast. They heard these 120 people, who had no reason to know other languages, now speaking in many different languages. That would be like hearing people talking in English, French, Russian, Spanish, and German all at the same time. The people were very surprised and confused, yet it meant *everyone* could understand what the 120 were saying!

What was happening?

Peter stood up and told the people that many years earlier, the prophet *Joel* said this day would come—when God would pour out His Spirit on all people—old and young, men and women.

Today that prophecy was coming true!

Now Peter felt the *power* of the Holy Spirit helping him to be bold and tell all the people that Jesus came to earth to die for their sins, that He rose again, and that He is now back in heaven with God the Father. Peter also told them that on that special day of Pentecost, God had given them the power of the Holy Spirit.

The people felt the awfulness of their sins and asked Peter, *"What shall we do?"*

Peter answered with boldness,

"Change your life. Turn to God and be baptized, each of you, in the name of Jesus Christ, so your sins are forgiven. Receive the gift of the Holy Spirit. The promise is targeted to you and your children, but also to all who are far away—whomever, in fact, our Master God invites."

And that day, 3,000 people became part of God's Kingdom.

Would you like to be part of God's Kingdom?

Just say:

"Father God, thank You for sending Your Son Jesus to die on the cross for my sins. Please forgive me for all the wrong things I have done. I want to be in Your Kingdom. Thank You that Your Holy Spirit now lives inside me to help me. Now I ask You to also baptize me with the Holy Spirit, so I will be bold and not afraid to tell others about You and Your Kingdom. Please show me Your dream for me. In Jesus' Name, I ask this. Amen."

Welcome to God's Kingdom!

As we discussed on pages 46 and 47, it is important to be baptized in water to show others that you have decided to be in God's Kingdom.

You will want to take Holy Communion to remember that Jesus died for us. The bread reminds us of His body being beaten so our bodies can be well. The cup (juice from grapes) reminds us of His blood that was poured out so we can be forgiven of our sins and be protected from evil.

Remember, you will always be in God's Kingdom
—here on earth now—
and in heaven when you die.

Now let's get back to what's happening with the disciples!

After the disciples were *baptized* with the Holy Spirit, they received the *power* Jesus had promised. That word "power" is from the same word we get "dynamite." That's really strong power!

The disciples started sharing all that Jesus had taught them. More and more people chose God's Kingdom every day. People were healed, even as the disciples walked by them. The disciples started sharing with each other and caring for those who were poor.

And they now spoke in heaven-given languages. They could be called *"the language of the Kingdom."*

Do you remember that the governor of the Roman Empire taught all the people in that kingdom to speak the same Roman language?

When we speak in our heaven-given languages, *we are speaking the language of God's Kingdom!*

Even though we don't understand the words we're saying, the Holy Spirit inside us understands perfectly what needs to be said to God the Father in heaven.

On page 26, we learned about some people who decided to build a tall tower. *God saw that they would be able to do anything they wanted because they spoke the same language.* So, God had them talk in different languages so they couldn't understand each other or finish the tower.

But now the Holy Spirit gives us the power to speak in heaven-given languages, and *it's all the same language!* That means we now have the power to do many wonderful things in God's Kingdom because we are able to communicate clearly with God the Father and He with us.

It is actually very natural for God's people to speak heaven-given languages!

When we pray, it is good to talk to God the Father in our heaven-given language more than in the language spoken in our country. That way, the Holy Spirit is able to help us pray according to God's will.

It gets even better!

The Holy Spirit also gave the disciples (and you!) very special gifts.

We call these gifts *"The Gifts of the Spirit."* That means they are *given* to us by the Holy Spirit. They are special presents that we must value and treat with great care. They are *not* medals or trophies that we have earned in some way.

Unlike the presents you receive on your birthday or at Christmas that you might keep just for yourself, these *Gifts of the Spirit* are to be used to help others in God's Kingdom.

They are NOT for you to keep for yourself and brag about.

In fact, God's dream for you will always include helping others. That's what being part of God's Kingdom is all about!

~REMEMBER~
God's gifts are to be shared,
not bragged about.

Do you remember the *"Fruit of the Spirit"* on page 61?

Love
Joy
Peace
Patience
Kindness
Goodness
Faithfulness
Gentleness
Self-control

It is very important you let these get strong in you because they are the nature of God. That means God doesn't just show love; it means God *is* Love.

You must first let the Holy Spirit teach you how to be loving, kind, and gentle—then you will take good care of the gifts we are going to talk about.

Even though we don't yet live in another Garden of Eden where everything is perfect, we must let the Holy Spirit teach us how to live according to God's Kingdom in this not-so-perfect world!

Now, let's talk about these nine special *"Gifts of the Spirit."*

The Holy Spirit gave three gifts that have to do with speech:

1) Prophecy
If the Holy Spirit encourages you to prophesy, that means you will feel God the Father wants you to say something that will encourage or comfort someone.

Perhaps you will go to a friend and say, "I feel God wants you to know how much He loves you and that He is going to help you not to feel lonely."

2) Different kinds of heaven-given languages
The Holy Spirit may want you to speak in a heaven-given language when you are with other people. It may be a language someone else will understand even though you don't.

Perhaps you are with some people, and you feel words forming in your mind. When it is a polite time to speak, you speak those words in a heaven-given language.

3) The interpretation of heaven-given languages
The Holy Spirit may give you the interpretation, or understanding, of what was spoken in the unknown language (as in #2).

Perhaps the Holy Spirit will give you or someone else the meaning of what you said in your heaven-given language so the other people will understand.

The Holy Spirit gave three gifts that have to do with power:

4) The Gift of Faith
The Holy Spirit may give you a special confidence to believe something, like a miracle, will happen.

Perhaps you will feel strongly that your friend who is sick with cancer will be healed.

5) Gifts of Healing
The Holy Spirit may want you to pray for someone to be healed without the use of medicine or surgery.

Perhaps you will go and pray for your sick friend, and he will be healed—even though he didn't even know God heals!

6) Gift of Miracles
The Holy Spirit may want to use you to do something that is more than a healing—it's totally impossible!

Perhaps you have a crowd of people at your house. They are hungry, and you don't have enough food for all of them. But you pray, and suddenly the food keeps appearing and lasts until everyone has eaten all they want! And you just know that was a miracle!

The Holy Spirit gave three gifts that show something:

7) Word of Wisdom
The Holy Spirit may give you information directly from God about something.

Perhaps you will feel you should take your coat with you to school even though the sun is shining, and the forecast predicts a warm day. But the weather turns cold, and you are glad you brought your coat!

8) Word of Knowledge
The Holy Spirit may let you know certain facts directly from God.

Perhaps you will feel the Holy Spirit wants you to pray for someone immediately because something is wrong. You pray and later find out he escaped being in an accident.

9) Discerning of Spirits
The Holy Spirit may let you know what is an evil spirit and what is a good spirit.

Perhaps you will walk into a room and suddenly feel that something is wrong. You tell Satan to leave, and he must go. Then a peaceful feeling comes over you, and you feel happy again.

Why does the Holy Spirit give us such special gifts?

Remember, the Holy Spirit is in constant communication with God the Father to know exactly how God wants His Kingdom on earth to operate.

Now the Holy Spirit wants to show you exactly what God the Father wants you to do as you live in His Kingdom! And He has given you all these gifts so you can help others.

God wants you to be very happy in His Kingdom!

Go back to the first part of this book and read again about Adam and Eve in the Garden of Eden. God wants to trust you with the same happy life that Adam and Eve enjoyed in the Garden of Eden.

Can He trust you?

Will you be God's friend and love Him and talk to Him?

Will you listen when He wants to talk to you?

Will you obey Him when He asks you to do something?

Will you be responsible to—
obey your parents?
be kind to your family and friends?
keep a clean room?
do your schoolwork?
take care of your dog?

Do you remember how the Roman Empire sent a governor to live among the people to teach them the ways of the kingdom? (See page 31.)

*God sent the Holy Spirit
back to the earth to be our Governor
and live in our hearts to teach us
the ways of God's Kingdom.*

God gave us power over sin and sickness!

*God gave us the privilege of speaking
the same language!*

God gave us gifts to help each other!

*Now enjoy being part of God's Kingdom
and living His dream for your life!*

*⁓ALWAYS REMEMBER⁓
God loves you*

SCRIPTURE REFERENCES

pp. 1-4: Genesis 1:1-26; 1 Chronicles 29:11; Psalms 24:1-2; 33:6-9; 89:11; 95:3-5; 104:5-31; 119:89-91; 121:1; 124:8; 134:3; 146:5-6; 147:4-9; 148:1-14; Hebrews 11:3; Revelation 4:11

p. 5: 1 Chronicles 28:9; Job 42:2; Psalms 103:19; 139:1-18; 147:4-5; Proverbs 15:3; Isaiah 66:1; Matthew 10:30; Revelation 19:6

p. 6: Psalm 29:10; Matthew 6:9; John 14:1-4; 1 Corinthians 2:9; Revelation 22:1-5

pp. 7-8: Psalms 91:11-12; 103:20-21; Isaiah 6:1-3; Daniel 10:10-21; 12:1; Matthew 1:20; 2:13; 4:11; 16:27; 28:2; Luke 1:19, 26; 2:8-14; Acts 1:10-11; 8:26; 1 Thessalonians 4:16; Hebrews 1:14; 12:22; Jude 9; Revelation 1:1; 12:7

pp. 9-10: Isaiah 14:12-15; Ezekiel 28:13-15; 2 Peter 2:4; 1 John 3:8; Revelation 12:4,7,9; 20:10

p. 11: Genesis 1:1-26; Psalms 89:11; 115:14-18

p. 12: Isaiah 42:5; 1 Thessalonians 5:23

p. 13: Genesis 1:26-30; 2:1-8; Psalms 8:6-9; 115:15-16

p. 14: Genesis 2:8-9, 15-17

p. 15: Genesis 2:18, 21-23

p. 16: Genesis 1:31

p. 17: Genesis 2:1-3

p. 18: Psalms 148; 150:6

p. 19: Genesis 3:1-5

pp. 20-24: Genesis 2:15-17; 3:1-24

p. 25: Exodus 9:29; 19:5; Deuteronomy 10:14; Psalm 115:15-16

p. 26: Genesis 4-9; 11:1-9

p. 27: Genesis 12:1-3; Leviticus 17:11; Deuteronomy 9:5

p. 28: Numbers 33:50-56; Judges 2:1-23; 3:6; Ruth 4:11, 22

p. 29: Isaiah 9:6-7; 40:3; Daniel 7:13-14; Micah 5:2

p. 30: Psalms 22:1,7-8, 16-18; 41:9; Isaiah 53:3-12; Zechariah 9:9; 11:12-13; 12:10; Revelation 1:7

p. 31: Luke 2:1-5

pp. 32-33: Luke 1:5-23

pp. 34-37: Psalm 139:13-18; Luke 1:24-80

p. 38: Matthew 1:18-25

pp. 39-40: Luke 2:1-20; Galatians 4:4-5

pp. 41-44: Leviticus 12:1-8; Micah 5:2; Matthew 2:1-23; 3:11; Mark 1:1-13; Luke 2:22-52

pp. 45-47: Deuteronomy 8:3; Matthew 3:1-17; John 1:19-34

pp. 48-49: Deuteronomy 6:13,16; 8:3; 10:20; Joshua 24:14; Psalm 91:11-12; Matthew 4:1-11; Luke 4:1-15; John 3:26-30; James 4:7

p. 50: Matthew 4:23-25; 5:1-2; 14:13-21; 19:13-15; 26:37; Mark 1:35; Mark 3:14-19; 9:2; Luke 6:12-16; 8:1; John 5:19; 8:28-29; 12:49-50

p. 51: Matthew 8:23-27; 17:14-18; 22:36-40; Mark 4:35-41; 9:14-27; Mark 12:30-31; Luke 8:22-25

p. 52: Matthew 6:9-13

pp. 53-54: Exodus 12:1-28; Matthew 26:6-13; Mark 14:3-9; John 12:1-8; 13:1-17; Hebrews 9:22

p. 55: Matthew 21:1-11; 26:17-29; Mark 11:1-11; 14:12-25; Luke 19:29-40; 21:14-23; John 12:12-19

p. 56: Matthew 26:20-25; John 14:1-6, 16-18

p. 57: Matthew 26:14-16, 39; Mark 15:16-47; Luke 22:3-6, 42; 23:44-56; John 19:30; 2 Corinthians 5:21; Philippians 2:8-11; Hebrews 9:22

pp. 58-60: Matthew 28:1-20; Mark 16:1-20; Luke 24:1-53; John 20:1-29; 21:1-25; Acts 1:1-11

p. 61: John 15:2; Galatians 5:22-23

pp. 62-65: Isaiah 53:5; Acts 2:1-39; Romans 10:9-10; 1 Corinthians 11:23-25; Philippians 2:9-11; Colossians 1:14; 1 Peter 2:24

pp. 66-73: Psalm 84:11; Luke 12:32; 1 Corinthians, chapters 12-14

CPSIA information can be obtained
at www.ICGtesting.com
Printed in the USA
LVHW011654270821
696212LV00006B/14